Art's Way—

" *If you are going to go, go First Class.* **"**

" *Compassion is the Greatest Gift.* **"**

Mission Statement

The Baltimore Ravens Mission is to win football games.

We can only achieve our mission if we are a team of people aspiring

to be the leading professional sports and entertainment company.

Setting the standard in competition, customer satisfaction and

business practices is our imperative.

Here, the extraordinary must be commonplace.

Stephen A. Burch
President
Mid-Atlantic Division
Comcast

Comcast congratulates the World Champion Baltimore Ravens on their historic 2000 season. Comcast is proud to be a major partner of the Baltimore Ravens, as we work together to set the standard of excellence in providing world-class sports entertainment and customer service to sports fans throughout Maryland and the entire Mid-Atlantic area.

SUPER JOURNEY

DIARY OF THE RAVENS
WORLD CHAMPIONSHIP SEASON

BALTIMORE RAVENS
Editors/Writers Kevin Byrne, Francine Gerres Lubera
Photography Phil Hoffmann (except where noted)

NFL PUBLISHING
Editor-in-Chief John Wiebusch
General Manager Bill Barron
Executive Editor Tom Barnidge
Managing Editor John Fawaz
Super Journey **Art Director** Bill Madrid
Assistant Art Director Jim Hudgens
Director-Photo Services Paul Spinelli
Photo Editor Kevin Terrell
Manager-Photo Services Tina Resnick
Director-Manufacturing Dick Falk
Director-Print Services Tina Dahl

FOREWORD
BY ART MODELL

Only 15 franchises have won Super Bowls in the game's 35-year existence. It's an elite group, and we're excited to be on that list. Beyond that, we're thrilled for members of our Ravens' family, Baltimore area fans and others throughout Maryland who have supported us during our first five seasons. Winning Super Bowl XXXV ended a memorable season that had us and our fans at the edge of our seats, standing in aisles and parading in downtown Baltimore.

Many years ago, my friend Edward Bennett Williams, a great attorney and owner of the Orioles, talked about the power of a sports franchise to a community. We agreed that no other force could coalesce the people of an area more than a winning team. No politician, teacher or minister can unify a community like the home team. The energy created by the Ravens winning the Super Bowl was magic to Baltimore and Maryland. All levels of society joined the celebration. Rich cheered side by side with poor, with nationality and religion not a factor. There was unity created as fans prodded us along and then celebrated our victories. It was thrilling to watch this all come together.

This Super Bowl diary will stimulate memories of great football

plays in our Super Bowl drive. And I'll enjoy looking back at some of the great games, such as the home victory over the Jaguars and the road wins at Tennessee and Oakland, but I'll especially remember the fans. The fans at PSINet Stadium with their overwhelming support, the overflow crowd greeting us at BWI Airport upon our return following the November win against the Titans, and the incredible crowd at our victory parade in 35-degree weather and pouring rain—all come to mind.

And with all the victories and the championship, I'll also remember tears from the Baltimore Ravens' championship season. We had tears of joy, of pride, and of thanks. I cried when I addressed the team after the Super Bowl win. Trent Dilfer's tears of pure joy in Tennessee after that heart-pounding comeback during the regular season were beautiful. Jermaine Lewis pointing to the sky with eyes glistening on his two punt returns for touchdowns against the Jets will never be forgotten, nor will Brian Billick welling up when he saw the airport crowd after the Tennessee game.

Enjoy this diary of our Super Bowl journey. May it stir fond memories, bring smiles, and maybe a few tears of joy.

INTRODUCTION

The Baltimore Ravens' Super Journey had so many elements. It's a championship story featuring a history-making defense, team and personal comebacks, outstanding leadership, and coming of age. It's also about good people giving of themselves to benefit a team and a community. There were heroes on the field, in the front office, and in the stands.

The Ravens were not an overnight success, and this is not simply a story about a roster filled with gifted players and a talented head coach. It's about hiring the right people to assemble the team. It's about bringing Brian Billick to Baltimore, and it's about the coaching staff he assembled. It's about Ozzie Newsome and the personnel experts who built a championship squad. It's about key player additions such as Shannon Sharpe and Jamal Lewis. It's about Goose, Rod, Matt, and Rob. It's about all of those elements and more.

The Ravens' Super Journey began with an ominous regular-season schedule that included five road games in seven weeks. After shutting out the Steelers in the final season opener at Three Rivers Stadium, the Ravens came home to face the Jaguars, a team Baltimore had never beaten. Trailing 23-7 at halftime, Billick told his team: "Win or lose, how we react in the second half will go a long way to determining what kind of team we become." The Ravens' fans will long remember that comeback victory.

There were other critical points on the Journey. The Ravens went five games without a touchdown, but the drought never divided the team. Nor did it dampen playoff hopes, thanks to a record-setting defense. The

sputtering offense necessitated a quarterback change, and that move quickly paid off with a comeback at Tennessee, as the Ravens became the first visiting NFL team to win at Adelphia Coliseum.

The Journey is about a defense that allowed the fewest points ever in a 16-game season. Ray Lewis earned NFL defensive player of the year honors. Rod Woodson and Sam Adams joined him with Pro Bowl seasons. The defensive line stopped the run and harassed quarterbacks while entertaining fans and tormenting opponents.

Overcoming obstacles was a central theme along the Journey: Ray Lewis rebounding from a trying offseason; Dilfer returning to Tampa for the Super Bowl; and Jermaine Lewis dedicating an emotional performance to the memory of his stillborn son. The team demonstrated its character during dramatic comebacks against Jacksonville, Tennessee, and the Jets.

The Journey is about leadership and coming of age. When the going got tough, veterans such as Rod Woodson, Ray Lewis, Rob Burnett and Shannon Sharpe stood tallest. Jamal Lewis, young cornerbacks Chris McAlister and Duane Starks, and Mike Flynn all proved that they were up to the challenges thrown in their paths.

In the end, the Journey is also about good players giving great effort. It's about the Modells, a lifelong football family, sharing a dream season with the Baltimore community. And it's about that community, index fingers raised, embracing their world championship team.

Contents

"This is my fortieth NFL season of ownership, and this is the best defense I've had. Our offense will be improved. But, I'm not printing playoff tickets yet. Lots of things can happen, including injuries. We have, however, put ourselves in a position to win now."
—Art Modell

THE JOURNEY BEGINS

> **Here's my sleeper team in the AFC: I'm picking the Ravens for the Super Bowl.**
> —Cris Collinsworth, FOX analyst

> **If there's a Cinderella story in the NFL this year, I think it's probably the Ravens.**
> —Hub Arkush, *Pro Football Weekly*

> **Winning all of our preseason games is a good thing. You gain nothing from losing.**
> —Brian Billick

Al Messerschmidt

The Ravens entered training camp brimming with confidence, thanks to one of the NFL's best defenses and veteran signal-callers Tony Banks (12, above) and Trent Dilfer (8). Fierce competition characterized two-a-days (left), while players such as fullback Obafemi Ayanbadejo (right) propelled Baltimore to preseason victories over Philadelphia, the Jets, Carolina, and the Giants. The Ravens opened the regular season by playing five of their first seven games on the road. Coach Billick called it "The Journey."

September 3: Ravens 16, Steelers 0 at Three Rivers Stadium. Rod Woodson (26), who played 10 seasons for the Steelers, paid his last visit to Three Rivers on a day when the Ravens' defense manhandled the Steelers (223 total yards). Qadry Ismail caught seven passes for 102 yards, including a 53-yard touchdown, and Matt Stover kicked three field goals to supply Baltimore's scoring.

> *I believe the toughest game in all of professional sports is for the road team to win in the NFL, but I knew we could win in Pittsburgh. We did it the year before. We just didn't expect the shutout.*
> —Brian Billick

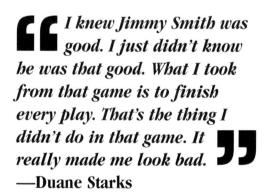 September 10: Ravens 39, Jaguars 36 at PSINet Stadium. One of the most exciting games of the 2000 NFL season brought Brian Billick and Tony Siragusa (above) onto the field and brought a dance from Jamie Sharper (right). Tony Banks rallied the Ravens from a 17-0 deficit by passing for 262 yards and a career-high five touchdowns. Trailing 36-32 with 1:45 left, Banks led the Ravens 75 yards to the winning score on his 29-yard pass to Shannon Sharpe.

" *I knew Jimmy Smith was good. I just didn't know he was that good. What I took from that game is to finish every play. That's the thing I didn't do in that game. It really made me look bad.* **"**
—Duane Starks

It took Hurricane Gordon, high winds, an emotional tribute to Dan Marino, and the Dolphins to snap the Ravens' two-game winning streak.

September 17: Dolphins 19, Ravens 6 at Pro Player Stadium. Miami's defense sacked Tony Banks (12) six times during a stormy night in south Florida. The loss deprived the Ravens of the first 3-0 start in their history.

Rob Burnett's crushing tackle on Akili Smith sidelined him early in the second quarter. The Bengals crossed midfield only three times in the game.

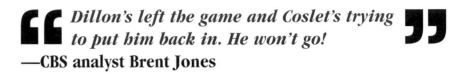
" Dillon's left the game and Coslet's trying to put him back in. He won't go! "
—CBS analyst Brent Jones

September 24: Ravens 37, Bengals 0 at PSINet Stadium. Jamal Lewis (above) ran for 116 yards in his first NFL start, and Rob Burnett (right) and the Ravens' defense held Cincinnati to 94 total yards, including only nine yards on 12 carries by Corey Dillon.

With two shutouts in the first four games, the mind set of the defense was, as Ray Lewis put it at Friday's practice: "No one should score a touchdown on us. No one. Does everybody understand?" The Browns moved into the red zone three times in the shutout loss to the Ravens, including twice in the fourth quarter. Each time the Browns got inside the 20, Ray's defensive mates showed they understood.

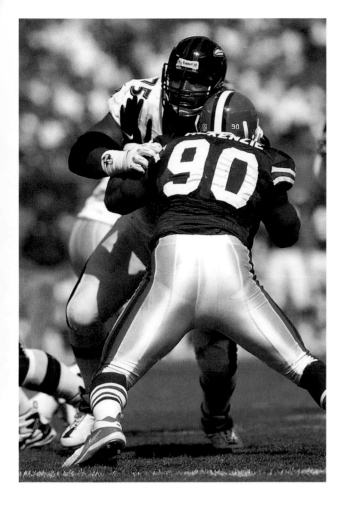

You go on the road against a damn good team that is absolutely desperate. A desperate team willing to give up anything to get a win. And you get a win on the road, and it's been a long road for us, guys. There's something special going on. We gotta build on it.
—Brian Billick

October 1: Ravens 12, Browns 0 at Cleveland Browns Stadium. Behind Jonathan Ogden (above) and the offensive line, Baltimore powered its way to 188 rushing yards. Peter Boulware (left) and the defense did the rest as the Ravens became the first team since the 1985 Chicago Bears to post consecutive shutouts.

October 8: Ravens 15, Jaguars 10 at ALLTEL Stadium. No shootout this time, as Baltimore used the same formula that worked against the Browns to win at Jacksonville in prime time. Matt Stover kicked five field goals to supply all of the Ravens' points for the second consecutive week, while Ray Lewis (right) and the defense recorded three sacks and forced six turnovers.

Voices raised, fingers pointed. There were stares. Two got nose-to-nose. There was frustration and some fatigue. There was some nasty. It was in the offensive coaches' meeting in Cavanaugh's office.

October 15: Redskins 10, Ravens 3 at FedEx Field. On a hard-hitting day, Jamie Sharper and Duane Starks (below) swarmed James Thrash, and an intense Michael McCrary (right) pursued a Redskins' ball carrier. The Ravens failed to score a touchdown for the third straight game, only this time it cost them as Washington's Stephen Davis ran 33 yards for the winning score early in the fourth quarter.

" *We were not scoring touchdowns. We're all very competitive. We weren't in there patting each other on the back. We had to find answers. Yeah, we argued. We got angry with each other. We needed answers.*
—Matt Cavanaugh "

It was obvious by the time the Titans came to PSINet for game eight that they were the team to beat in the AFC Central. The Ravens' defense proved that it could handle Eddie George; it was Steve McNair that worried the Ravens' coaches. "He makes at least one broken play a game that kills us," defensive line coach Rex Ryan said.

October 22: Titans 14, Ravens 6 at PSINet Stadium. The Ravens outplayed the Titans—and still lost. Shannon Sharpe (left) caught eight passes for 104 yards, and the offense amassed 368 yards. Nevertheless, Baltimore's touchdown-less streak reached four weeks, and its losing streak reached two, as Tennessee parlayed an interception into the game's only touchdown. The Ravens' defense, on the other hand, continued to perform magnificently. Rod Woodson (above) and company held the Titans to 191 total yards and seven first downs.

It was time to change the starter at quarterback and Brian Billick did it in his typical blunt and honest style. Bringing Trent Dilfer and Tony Banks into his office, Brian said: "Both of you should hear the same thing. Trent, you're the starter. Tony, I'm going to give Trent the same support I gave you. This is no experiment. Trent is the starter until he tells us he can't make the plays for us to win."

October 29: Steelers 9, Ravens 6 at PSINet Stadium. Trent Dilfer (above) took over at quarterback, but the touchdown drought reached five games despite the determined efforts of tackle Jonathan Ogden and tight end Ben Coates (right). The losing streak also continued, reaching three games, but Dilfer and the Ravens would not lose again.

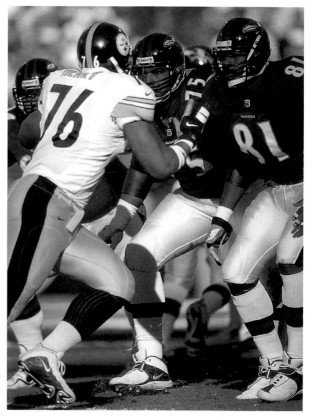

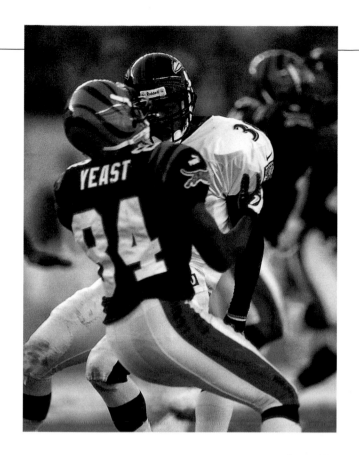

> *What makes this season so exhilarating is the five-game touchdown drought. I refer to it as the 'Dust Bowl.' To Brian's credit, and the credit of the organization and the players, we fought our way out of it. No one pointed fingers. This is a good team, and we're going to get better.*
> —Art Modell

November 5: Ravens 27, Bengals 7 at Paul Brown Stadium. It's over! The Ravens found the end zone for the first time since September when Trent Dilfer completed a 14-yard touchdown pass to Brandon Stokley (right) early in the second quarter. That opened the floodgate, as Dilfer found Shannon Sharpe for two more touchdown passes in the quarter to give Baltimore a 24-0 halftime lead. James Trapp (above) and the Ravens were back to their intimidating selves, serving notice on the AFC.

Trent Dilfer threw what he called "an idiot pass." Titans safety Perry Phenix grabbed it and raced 87 yards for a touchdown and a 23-17 Tennessee lead with 2:30 left in the game. After the chase, Trent had a 40-yard walk back to the bench. "In the first ten yards, I beat myself up. We had guys fighting as hard as they could out there, and I gave the game to Tennessee. In the second ten yards, I started to slap myself around. 'You have to snap out of it.' In the last twenty yards I rallied. 'Pick yourself up. We can win this game. I can make the plays to help make it happen.'" And Trent did.

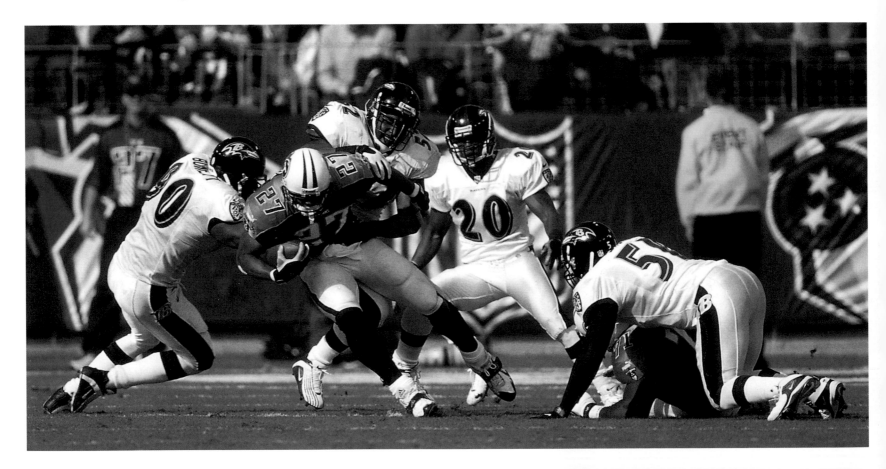

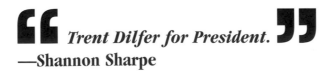 November 12: Ravens 24, Titans 23 at Adelphia Coliseum. Baltimore's defense shut down Eddie George (above), limiting him to 28 yards on 12 carries, but the Ravens still had to sweat out a close one at Tennessee. Trailing 23-17 in the final minutes, Trent Dilfer guided the Ravens 70 yards to the winning touchdown with 25 seconds left. Dilfer (right) then watched from the sideline as the Titans almost pulled off a last-second miracle.

" *Trent Dilfer for President.* "
—Shannon Sharpe

November 19: Ravens 27, Dallas 0 at PSINet Stadium. Jamal Lewis soared while the Ravens posted their fourth shutout of 2000.

When reporters evaluated the Ravens' draft, many proclaimed that Baltimore "reached" with the fifth overall pick. Others wrote that the Ravens took the wrong guy, that there were better backs such as Virginia's Thomas Jones, Wisconsin's Ron Dayne, and Alabama's Shaun Alexander. Against Dallas, that fifth overall pick, 21-year-old Jamal Lewis, powered his way for 187 rushing yards in a 27-0 demolition of America's Team.

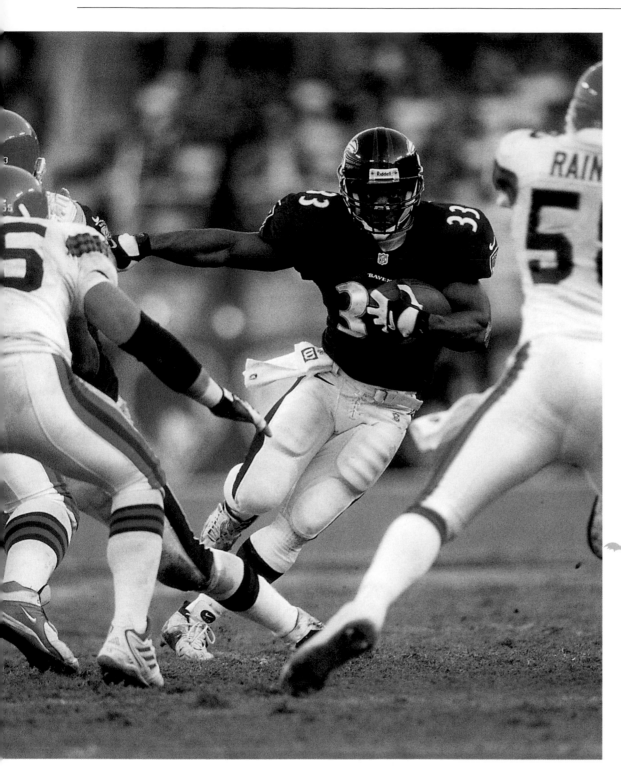

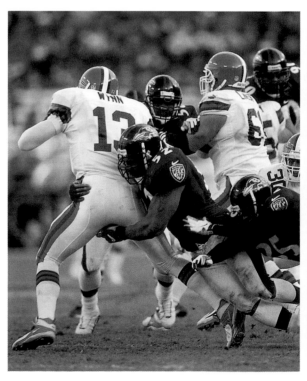

November 26: Ravens 44, Browns 7 at PSINet Stadium. Baltimore had six sacks against Cleveland, including one from Ray Lewis (below). Jamal Lewis gained 170 yards on 30 carries, and Priest Holmes (left) ran for the final score as the Ravens amassed 461 total yards while limiting Cleveland to 112.

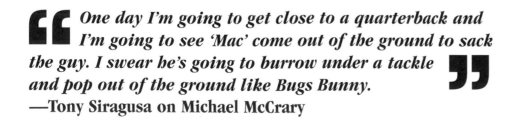

One day I'm going to get close to a quarterback and I'm going to see 'Mac' come out of the ground to sack the guy. I swear he's going to burrow under a tackle and pop out of the ground like Bugs Bunny.
—Tony Siragusa on Michael McCrary

"Obviously, the fine for the P-word is off! We earned the right to say we're a playoff team. We now have the right to say we want to go to the Super Bowl. No Festivus. No Festivus Maximus. Super Bowl."

—Brian Billick

December 10: Ravens 24, Chargers 3 at PSINet Stadium. Baltimore owner Art Modell (right) was introduced prior to the game to honor his fortieth year in the NFL, then watched his Ravens dismantle another opponent and thus secure the club's first playoff berth. The defense, coming off a bye week, produced another staggering performance (San Diego managed just 128 total yards and nine first downs) while the offense controlled the ball for nearly 38 minutes. After the game, Coach Billick (above) addressed the players in the locker room.

> **The doubts have got to end. McAlister and Starks have been showing up big time. Everyone who doubted them will have something to think about. They're the two best corners in the league.**
> —Sam Adams

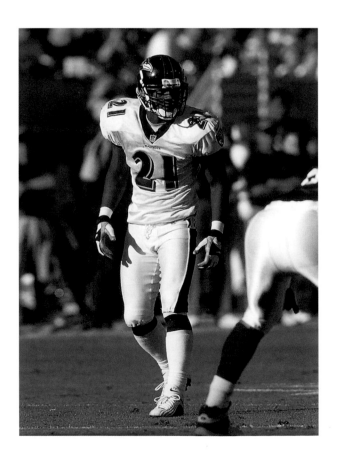

December 17: Ravens 13, Cardinals 7 at Sun Devil Stadium. Sam Adams (above), Chris McAlister (left), and the rest of Baltimore's defense shined again, stopping the Cardinals in the red zone with two minutes left to secure the Ravens' sixth consecutive victory. Baltimore forced four turnovers, and Jamal Lewis ran for 126 yards on 29 carries, including the Ravens' only touchdown on a one-yard run midway through the third quarter.

Brian Billick called Jermaine Lewis at home and told him not to go to Arizona for the game. "You need to be with your wife." Imara Lewis had just delivered prematurely, and their son was stillborn. When he returned for the Jets' game, Jermaine dedicated the game to his deceased son and responded with two punt returns for touchdowns. Each time Jermaine arrived in the end zone, he pointed to the sky and said, "This is for you."

December. 24: Ravens 34, Jets 20 at PSINet Stadium. In a wild season finale, New York outgained Baltimore 524-142, but thanks to a series of big plays, the Ravens overcame a 14-0 deficit and won the game. Jermaine Lewis (above) returned punts 89 and 54 yards for scores, Chris McAlister ran an interception back 98 yards for a touchdown, and Qadry Ismail (right) scored on a seven-yard pass. Baltimore's offense managed just 142 yards and five first downs, but the team tallied 486 return yards and forced six turnovers. Despite the rough day, the Ravens' defense still set an NFL mark for fewest points allowed (165) in a 16-game season.

" Sometimes when you fight through adversity, it just makes you better. It makes handling the good times more manageable because you know you have persevered. "
—Qadry Ismail

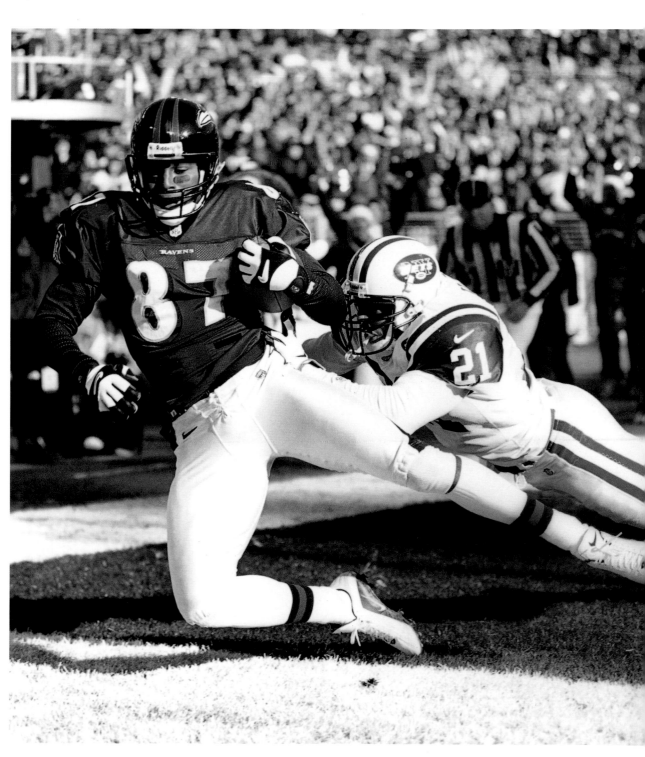

> *You play for a team. You fight for your family.*
> *We became a family as we went through the season.*
> —David Modell

comcast

FESTIVUS MAXIMUS

Every Thursday night since early in the season, Priest Holmes organized extra film-study sessions for the running backs at Jamal Lewis' house. "Priest, Sam Gash…they taught me how to be a professional. They also made me buy the food every week, because I was the rookie," Jamal said.

December 31: Ravens 21, Broncos 3 at PSINet Stadium, AFC Wild Card Game. Jamal Lewis helped the Ravens to a 7-0 lead with a 1-yard touchdown early in the second quarter. He went on to finish the game with 110 rushing yards on 30 carries.

> **We brought Shannon in here to make big plays and to get us to the playoffs. He's made some big plays, and we're in the playoffs.**
> —Ozzie Newsome

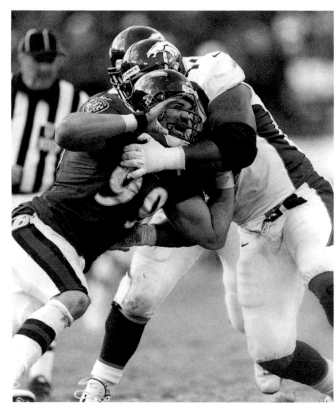

 A heads-up play by tight end Shannon Sharpe (left) turned a deflected pass into a 58-yard touchdown reception with less than five minutes left in the first half. A smothering defense, featuring three sacks by Michael McCrary (above right), and solid special-teams work took care of the rest.

❝ *If we do our jobs against those two 100-catch receivers, we win.* **❞**
—Duane Starks, before the playoff victory over Denver

❝ *Playoffs–it's either put up or shut up. That's what it really boils down to. Really.* **❞**
—Chris McAlister

❝ *At this point, when you get to the playoffs, you've got to be cocky. Let the other people know that, 'Hey, we're the team to beat.' Don't take anybody lightly. It's everybody's game. Make it yours.* **❞**
—Tony Siragusa

January 7: Ravens 24, Titans 10 at Adelphia Coliseum, AFC Divisional Playoff Game. Qadry Ismail, who led the Ravens with three receptions for 53 yards, provided a rare flash of offense on a day when yards were hard to come by.

Chris McAlister got caught. A *Sports Illustrated* article quoted him basically saying that Titans running back Eddie George had become reluctant to mix it up against the Ravens' defense. Some of his defensive teammates were on Chris when he ate breakfast in the players' lounge that Wednesday. Ray Lewis walked in and asked what was up. After hearing, he placed his hand on Chris' shoulder and said "I got your back."

" *Brian is very passionate. He's into the game and has a fire the guys like. We feed off his fuel. You know he is going to fight for you, and in turn we're going to fight for him. When they showed Brian on the (video)screens at the beginning of the game, it fired us up even more. We had to back* **"** *our coach.*
—Cornell Brown on Brian Billick

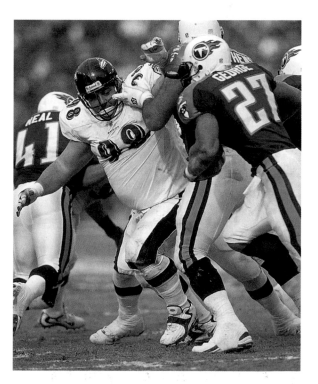

Keith Washington (93) delivered the biggest play of the game when he blocked a fourth-quarter field-goal attempt that Anthony Mitchell returned 90 yards for a touchdown. Ray Lewis (above) and Tony Siragusa spearheaded a defense that contributed seven points on Lewis' 50-yard interception return.

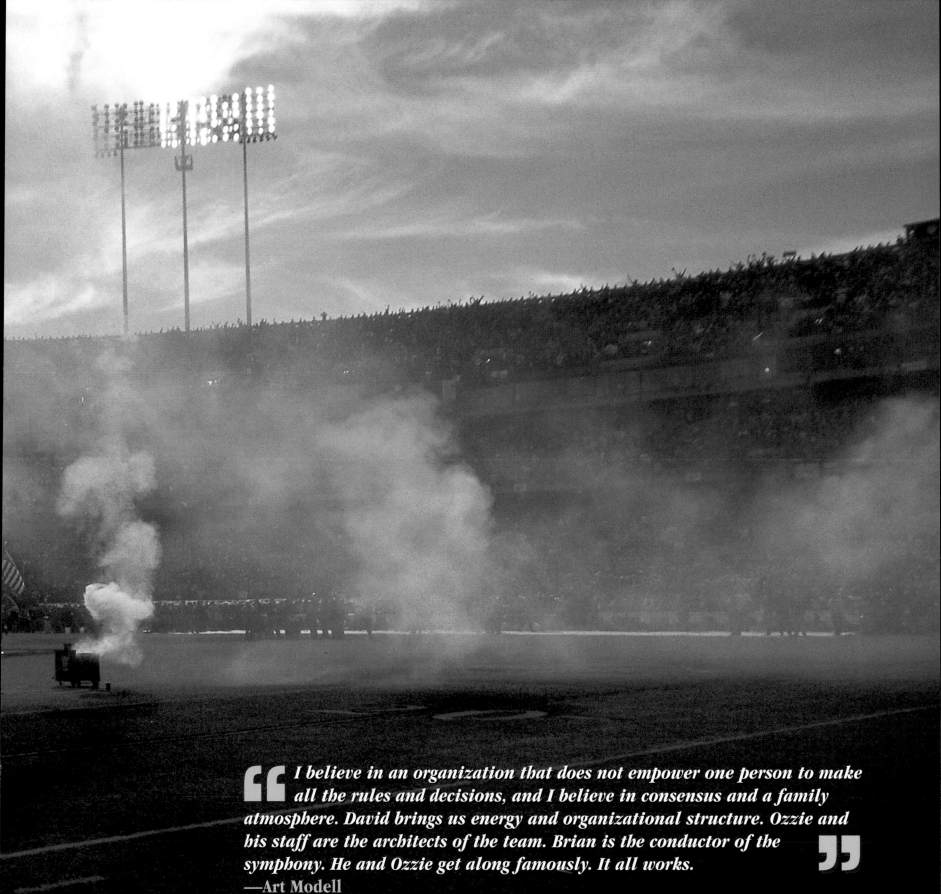

" *I believe in an organization that does not empower one person to make all the rules and decisions, and I believe in consensus and a family atmosphere. David brings us energy and organizational structure. Ozzie and his staff are the architects of the team. Brian is the conductor of the symphony. He and Ozzie get along famously. It all works.* "
—Art Modell

> *If that defense is not the best of all time, it's close to the top. They're very explosive from left to right corner; they're outstanding. They have a great pass rush with their front four with a lot of stunts. They force you to check the ball down at times, and when you do, there are guys like Ray Lewis and Jamie Sharper to rattle you. They don't give up many yards after the catch. That's the most impressive thing that I have seen from them. They are up there with the Fearsome Foursome and the Steel Curtain.*
> —Jon Gruden

January 14: Ravens 16, Raiders 3 at Network Associates Coliseum, AFC Championship Game. Michael McCrary and the Ravens' front line put relentless pressure on Raiders quarterback Rich Gannon, who was forced to leave the game.

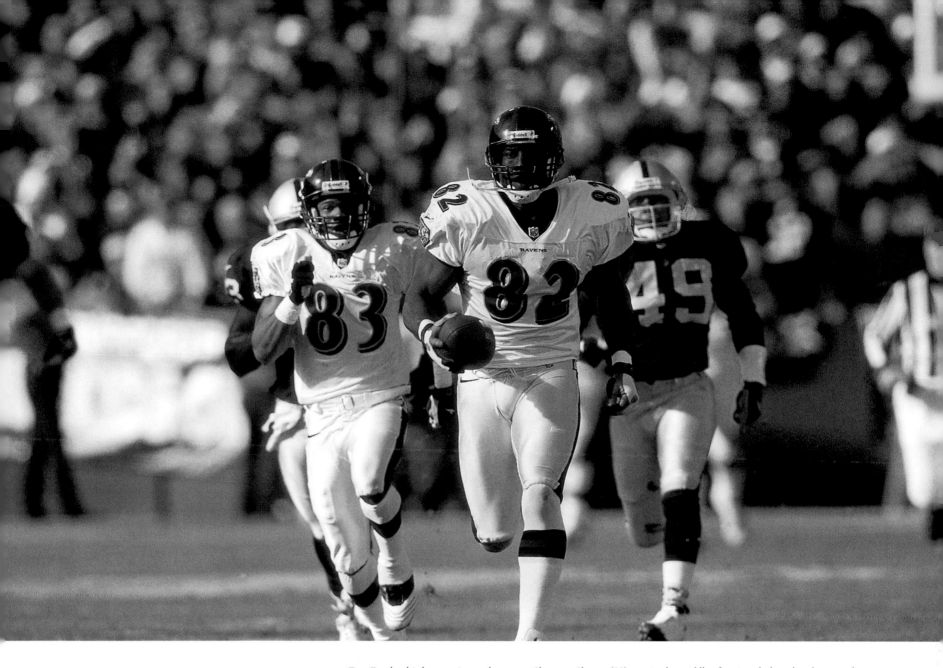

For the third successive week, veteran Shannon Sharpe (82) was in the middle of a pivotal play when he turned a short pass into a 96-yard touchdown for the first score of the game. Duane Starks (below) made his own special contribution with a pair of interceptions.

> **Now we're beginning to see the frustration in Jon Gruden with the Raiders unable to pick up 12 inches on this team.**
> —Greg Gumbel, CBS-TV

> **Marvin, how many points do you need from us today? 'Seven' was his reply.**
> —Shannon Sharpe

> **"** *Rob [Burnett] is the Dalai Lama. We go to him for answers. Sam [Adams] is Sybil. He has so many personalities. He switches quickly. One minute it's 'Hi Goose, how ya' doing?' The next it's 'Don't ever talk to me.' McCrary is the 'Boy in the Bubble.' He's weird and from another planet. Me? I'm the fat Italian guy from Jersey waiting for the cast call from* The Sopranos. **"**
> —Tony Siragusa

> **Baltimore, the whole world is watching. We're going to the Super Bowl!**
> —Shannon Sharpe

Smiles were in plentiful supply when the Ravens earned their first Super Bowl berth. At right, John (cap), David, and Art Modell accepted the Lamar Hunt Trophy from San Diego Chargers owner Alex Spanos. A short while later, Tony Siragusa, Lional (Jelly) Dalton, Rob Burnett, and Michael McCrary (bottom) showed off their new hardware.

Mike Moore

We need to take a lesson from the Ravens. We showed the rest of the world what Balitmore's about: persistence and resistance and being the best.
—Baltimore Mayor Martin O'Malley

BON VOYAGE

January 22: Tony Siragusa (above) and Ray Lewis address fans at a Super Bowl sendoff rally before leaving for Tampa.

❝ *If you're not excited, you don't have a pulse.* **❞**
—**Tony Siragusa**

❝ *What time is it? Game time. Are my dogs in the house? Woo! Woo! Woo!* **❞**
—**Ray Lewis**

Shortly after the rally, the Ravens' players, coaches, and staff boarded a charter flight to Tampa. Kicker Matt Stover, armed with a video recorder, documented the event.

> *I really do believe that when you get good, there's a certain synergy that happens between players, coaches, management, fans, and media that you can build on. If you've laid the groundwork, it will feed the team even more, and you'll go to even greater heights.*
> —Brian Billick

The AFC champions arrive in style in Tampa.

> *Before you ask any questions, I know the Giants will have a curfew. We will not. I know you are going to want to ask Ray and me a lot of questions. He answered all those questions last June. Just because someone wants to ask about it again doesn't mean that Ray or I, or any of the Ravens, have to address it again.*
> —Brian Billick

comcast

WELCOME TO TAMPA

January 23: During Super Bowl week, Tuesday means Media Day, which means lots of interviews—as Ray Lewis (above) and Art Modell (left) quickly discovered.

Approximately 2,000 of the 3,300 reporters covering the Super Bowl came to Raymond James Stadium on Tuesday to interview the Ravens. Prior to taking the field, the Ravens posed for shots that CBS would use to introduce the players during the game telecast. A team picture was taken after the one-hour media session.

Rod Woodson answered questions from a special interview kiosk, and the defensive line hammed it up on the field.

CBS had arranged to tape a pregame segment on Tuesday morning with Michael McCrary and his opposite number on the Giants, Lomas Brown. When reminded of the appointment, McCrary said: "I've changed my mind. I don't want to talk with my opponent before the game." McCrary reluctantly agreed to the interview, and when asked how it went, replied: "Lomas knows what his team is in for."

Michael McCrary (above) gave as good as he got when cameramen arrived, and Jamal Lewis (right) hardly seemed like a rookie in front of a gaggle of microphones.

A portrait of the artists who created a championship season.

At the end of Media Day, after the Super Bowl team player picture had been taken, Art and David asked all of the Ravens' associates attending the session to join them in a "real" team picture.

Tony Siragusa (above) and Jonathan Ogden (right) found themselves peppered with questions as the game approached, but they never were at a loss for words.

On Wednesday and Thursday of Super Bowl week, players talked to the media in huge tents located outside the team hotel.

Brad Jackson (left) found a novel way to get his face on the front page of the newspaper. Trent Dilfer (below) landed in the spotlight every day without even trying.

On Wednesday, Thursday, and Friday, the Ravens practiced at the University of South Florida. Coach Billick required all players to take the team buses to and from practice, and he was pleased when he heard Shannon Sharpe tell a teammate, "You can't ride back with your cousins. We ride as a team."

BEHIND THE SCENES

Chris McAlister wore the look of confidence as he departed the team bus for practice. And the mood was light for Art Modell and Ozzie Newsome (in cart), who shared a laugh with Pat Moriarty and James Harris.

> **I can help with regards to the demands of the league. I can help with the demands that you all [media] put on them. I can help them with the demands that the game puts on them. With their wives, sisters, brothers and cousins, they are on their own.**
> —Brian Billick

Brian Billick always found a way to maximize his time.

Jim Brown, believed by many to be the greatest player in NFL history, delivered a powerful message to the Ravens two days before the big game. "All of life is about accountability," Brown said. "On Sunday, you have to be accountable to yourself and your teammates. Every day you have to be accountable to your family and community. Be accountable, and you'll win the championship."

Pro Football Hall of Fame running back Jim Brown (above) and boxing legend Joe Frazier (left) each shared an inspirational message with the Ravens on Friday of Super Bowl week.

> **People can talk about our talent and speed on defense, but what stands out to me is our tackling. It's a lost art. We're good at it because the players work on it every single day. Even when we don't go live, we're getting in the right position to make tackles.**
> —Marvin Lewis on tackling

The Ravens attracted a flock of high-profile visitors as the clock ticked down on Super Bowl Sunday. CBS analyst Craig James talked with Marvin Lewis (top), baseball great Hank Aaron visited Art Modell (left), and movie director Spike Lee attempted a field goal.

> **He's got some work to do. Maybe Spike has spent too much time on free throws instead of extra points.**
> —Brian Billick

> *This team isn't tired. I think one of the main reasons is we got a lot of rest with the bye week. We really needed it after the West Coast trip. That one kind of hurt. I don't think we were beaten up, we were just a bit tired. But tired only goes so far. To be in a game like this, you get over it. With a game like this, I don't think you know what tired is.*
> **—Ray Lewis**

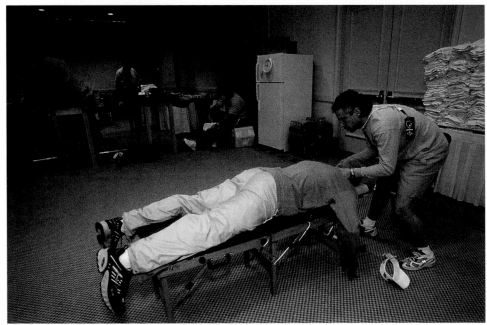

Assistant trainer Mark Smith tends to the treatment needs of Adalius Thomas (top), and Alan Sokoloff, one of the club's chiropractors, works out the kinks with Corey Harris.

The CBS crew met with selected players and coaches on Thursday to prepare for the game broadcast. Afterwards, commentator Phil Simms said: "Talk about confidence. These guys really believe they're going to win."

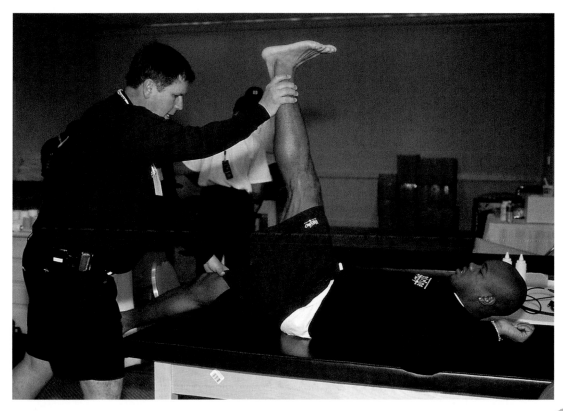

Head trainer Bill Tessendorf worked on Patrick Johnson (top), and assistant trainer Jeremy Sykes treated O.J. Brigance's ankle.

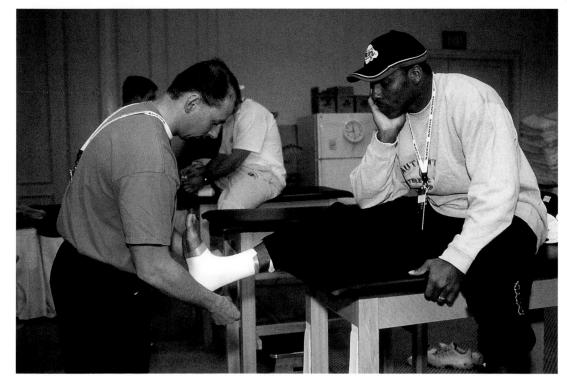

Shannon Sharpe demonstrated his skill with a cue stick for Earnest Byner, and Tony Banks tackled a video-game challenge.

> **" Their days here are occupied pretty well from the morning up to about 4 o'clock, much like it is during the regular season. After that, they are free to do what they normally do—turn 'em loose and hope they show good judgment. I think this group will. We've come this far. We'll keep their routines normal, something that makes them comfortable. "**
> —Brian Billick

While Tony Siragusa and strength coach Jeff Friday (below) relaxed with a game of foosball, Patrick Johnson and Shannon Sharpe (left) played ping pong.

Keeping with tradition and superstition, Baltimore Mayor Martin O'Malley delivered a familiar proclamation to Brian Billick. Below, the coach directed the Saturday walkthrough at Raymond James Stadium.

Each of the teams the Ravens defeated in the playoffs had won blowout games the previous week. Coach Billick's message after the Saturday practice: "Listen to me, guys. The Giants are just like the Broncos, Titans, and Raiders. They all won big before us and came in with confidence against us. The Giants don't respect us the way they should. You'll show them tomorrow what's real."

Nervous? Not the Ravens, who shared some laughs and took it easy the day before the Super Bowl. Even the club's minority owner, Steve Bisciotti (left, in the vest), joined in the fun.

A key to the Ravens' run at the NFL title was the coaching staff. "Marvin [Lewis] and Matt [Cavanaugh] are outstanding coordinators who will be head coaches," Billick said. "We have other assistants ready now to be coordinators and some of those will be head coaches. They are teachers and motivators. They work hard and smart."

After pregame warmups, Brian Billick and Ray Lewis stood outside the Ravens' locker room and talked privately for the first time all week. Ray offered: "Coach, they don't really know how good we are, do they?" Brian shook his head and said: "They're about to find out, Ray. They're about to find out."

NFLP/Kevin Terrell

comcast.

SUPER
BOWL
XXXV

Michael Zagaris

The Stealth Bomber flew overhead, Ray Charles (below) sang, and the Backstreet Boys (right) performed the National Anthem on the biggest day in Ravens history.

NFLP/Paul Spinelli

NFLP/Kevin Terrell

NFLP/Kevin Terrell

The Ravens told the NFL the order in which they wanted the defense introduced, starting with Goose and ending with Ray Lewis, who explained his pregame ritual: "My mind lets go and my body takes over. It's nothing that I anticipate or rehearse. I just go to another place, and my teammates and the fans feed off me."

The Ravens sacked Kerry Collins four times and hit him five other times during a game that he would rather forget.

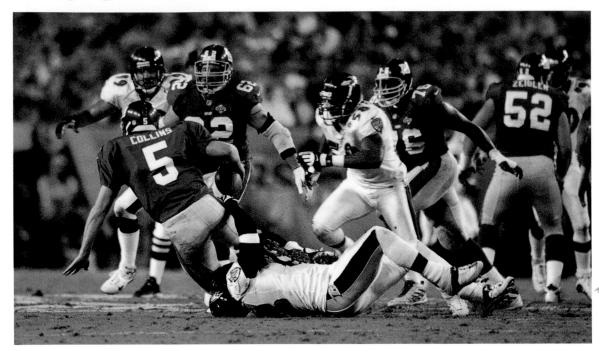

Giants quarterback Kerry Collins (left and below) received much more attention than he wanted. Ray Lewis (right) knocked away this pass intended for the Giants' Pete Mitchell.

❝ *We were watching film and noticed that when Collins was going to throw on timing routes on a three-step drop, he took a little hop on the second step. It let us anticipate some of his throws.* **❞**
—Duane Starks on intercepting Kerry Collins

❝ *Facing our defense is like having eleven billiard balls thrown at you.* **❞**
—Rob Burnett

Richard Mackson

> **On Wednesday of Super Bowl week, Dilfer predicted, 'Brandon will get into the end zone. You mark my words.'**
> —Joe Theismann, ESPN

Brandon Stokley, whose scoring catch ended the midseason touchdown drought, got the Ravens' first Super Bowl TD.

Al Messerschmidt

Brandon Stokley (above and right) got a step on the Giants' Jason Sehorn and hauled in a 38-yard touchdown pass for the first score in Super Bowl XXXV. Trent Dilfer (left) passed for 153 yards while winning his eleventh straight start.

> ❝ *When people watch us on film, they don't really watch what we do well, and that's fly to the ball. You're going to get seven, eight guys on the ball at all times. When we get on the field, and people see that, they go, 'Wow!'* ❞
> —**Ray Lewis**

> ❝ *A name for our defense? How about the best?* ❞
> —**Tony Siragusa**

The Ravens' defense dominated the Giants, just as they had dominated almost every other opponent during the 2000 season. Super Bowl XXXV MVP Ray Lewis (right) tallied five tackles and four passes defensed, while Tony Siragusa, Rob Burnett, and Lional Dalton (below) helped limit the Giants to 66 rushing yards. Cornerback Duane Starks (above) delivered a crushing blow when he picked off a pass from Kerry Collins and raced 49 yards for a touchdown that gave Baltimore a 17-0 third-quarter lead.

> ❝ *There is no chink in our armor from the front seven to the back four. We work as one.* ❞
> —**Chris McAlister**

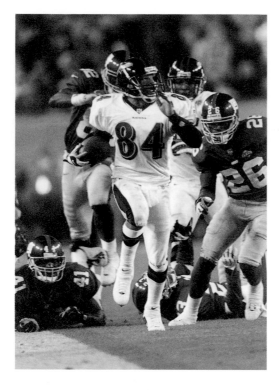

After the Giants scored on a kickoff return, Jermaine Lewis (right) answered with an electrifying 84-yard runback to give the Ravens a 24-7 lead. Jamal Lewis (below) scored on a three-yard run midway through the fourth quarter to increase Baltimore's advantage to 31-7.

Michael Zagaris

Jimmy Cribb

> **This game is all about intimidation. When I'm on the field, I'll do anything to show the other team that you don't want to mess with me. I use my power to break guys early. By the third and fourth quarters, when you're not so fresh, that's when I gash you.**
> —Jamal Lewis

> **Make history, Jay-Lew!**
> —Brian Billick

> **I knew we had them. I knew they were going to be tired. I think this was the dagger for them.**
> —Jermaine Lewis

Mitchell Reibel

> Jonathan Ogden (75) and the offensive line (above) cleared holes for Jamal Lewis, who ran for 102 yards. The Ravens' immovable object(s)—Tony Siragusa and Sam Adams—eschewed the high five in favor of a belly bounce (near right). After the game, Art Modell and the Ravens celebrated amidst a downpour of confetti (next page).

Mitchell Reibel

" *We know where our bread is buttered. We're not going to try to fool anybody, and everybody else knows it. Our job is not to lose it for those guys. We're going to play true to form. We're going to take care of the football. And if we get an opportunity to make some plays, we're going to make them. If not, we're going to live to see another day and punt the ball away.* "
—Shannon Sharpe

Amidst the pandemonium, the Modell family joined Brian Billick, Ozzie Newsome, and Ray Lewis on the victor's platform to accept the Vince Lombardi Trophy. Super Bowl XXXV was over. Art Modell celebrated his fortieth year in the NFL with the ultimate victory.

A jubilant Art Modell shared his thoughts with CBS announcer Jim Nantz (above), then shared the Vince Lombardi Trophy with the Ravens' players (right), including Jamie Sharper, Michael McCrary, and Peter Boulware, standing on the platform with David Modell's son Arthur and John Modell's son Dylan (wearing hat).

" *Here's an owner who comes to practice every day and asks us how we are. The first time he comes to the field is to get the AFC trophy and the next time is the Super Bowl. But he doesn't just hug me and Ray and Trent, he's hugging Poindexter and Mitchell and he knows their names. That speaks volumes. He cares about everybody.* **"**
—Shannon Sharpe on Art Modell

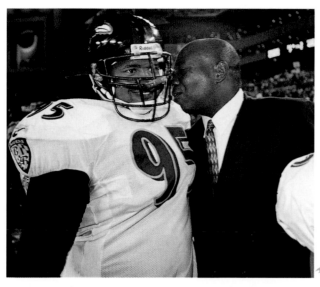

> **The key move was signing Shannon. That encouraged others to come. Getting Trent gave us a quality backup quarterback. The Sam Adams signing on draft day was very big. Drafting Jamal and Travis later that day took us to another level.**
> —**Ozzie Newsome**

Ozzie Newsome and Sam Adams (left) shared a hug. Brian Billick showed off the Ravens' new hardware.

It was surreal. You watched it all your life. The realization of this magnificent dream. There was noise and yelling all around you. Firecrackers going off, people embracing, shoving. You knew you were in a special place and moment. It may never happen again. But it was happening to you, right now.

Fans and media swarmed the field to celebrate or record the aftermath of Super Bowl XXXV.

Jonathan Ogden received congratulations from the Giants' Jessie Armstead (right), and then Raymond James Stadium turned into one big party for the Ravens and their fans.

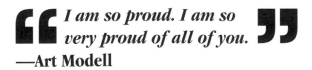 Art Modell talks to the World Champion Ravens following Baltimore's 34-7 victory over the New York Giants. At right, Modell and his wife Patricia in a private moment.

" *I am so proud. I am so very proud of all of you.* "
—Art Modell

David Modell celebrates in the locker room with Kathleen Kennedy Townsend, Maryland's Lieutenant Governor.

Stokley scored the game's first touchdown and explained what winning the Super Bowl meant to him and the Ravens.

This team taught me that the word 'team' is really just an extension of the word 'family,' and you are all part of that family.
—Brian Billick

comcast

WELCOME
HOME
CHAMPS

David Modell(right) showed the Vince Lombardi Trophy to fans at the Ravens' parade, which included a motorcade of Hummers and speeches from Ray Lewis and Brian Billick (below).

" *What superlative can I use to describe how great the fans were? If you want to define twelfth man, snap a picture of this crowd today, and put them in the diction-ary, because that's what they were. It was on their wings today. They did a great job.* **"**
—**David Modell**

It was in the low 30s, it was windy, and it was raining. "Should we ask the Mayor to cancel this thing? It's raining. No one will come." Art Modell was wrong on this one...More than 200,000 fans lined the streets of downtown Baltimore to salute their champions.

> **There's a lot of chemistry in this organization, a lot of love for each other. Vince Lombardi told me years and years ago that in order to win, you've got to love each other.**
> —Art Modell